MOMMY,

Someone's Touching Susan

Judith McClure and Sandra Moyle

Balboa Press books may be ordered through booksellers or by contacting:

Balboa Press
A Division of Hay House
1663 Liberty Drive
Bloomington, IN 47403
www.balboapress.com
1 (877) 407-4847

Because of the dynamic nature of the Internet, any web addresses or links contained in this book may have changed since publication and may no longer be valid. The views expressed in this work are solely those of the author and do not necessarily reflect the views of the publisher, and the publisher hereby disclaims any responsibility for them.

Any people depicted in stock imagery provided by Thinkstock are models, and such images are being used for illustrative purposes only.
Certain stock imagery © Thinkstock.

ISBN: 978-1-5043-7065-3 (sc)
ISBN: 978-1-5043-7066-0 (e)

Library of Congress Control Number: 2016919832

Print information available on the last page.

Balboa Press rev. date: 01/18/2017

BALBOA
PRESS
A DIVISION OF HAY HOUSE

"Mommy, Someone's Touching Susan" is a sensitive and helpful story written for children of all ages. Demonstrating their understanding of child development and psychology, the authors deliver an easy-to-ready story of child sexual abuse that provides children the permission they need to share a dark "Secret" with an adult. Only by sharing this secret can children begin the process of healing.

This beautifully illustrated book is an excellent addition to all family and public libraries that recognize the need for guidance – to the one out of ten children who will be sexually assaulted before the age of 18.

Helen B. Miller, PhD

Counselor and former Mayor, Town of White Springs, FL

Founder HOPE SUMMER ENRICHMENT PROGRAM

President, Suwannee River League of Cities

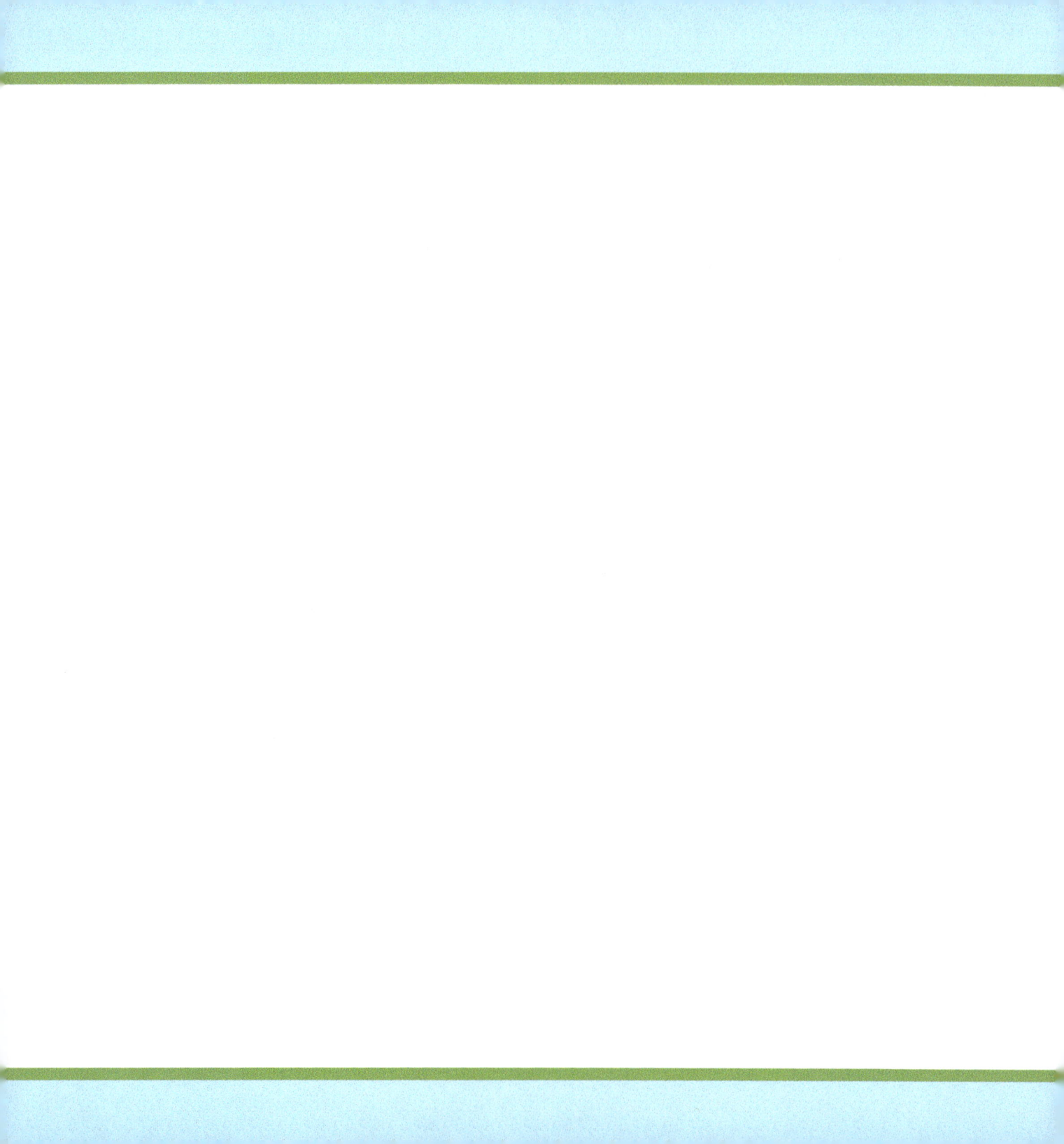

DEDICATED TO A GRANDDAUGHTER

Susan and Rosa were best friends. They shared everything, secrets and all. They rode the bus to school. At lunch they sat together. On rainy days they splashed in puddles and made mud pies. On weekends they made playhouses out of cardboard boxes and ate jelly sandwiches while catching bugs in tin cans. Everything was more fun when Susan and Rosa were together.

Then, one day things changed. It was right after Susan's uncle moved in with her and her mom. Just like that, Susan grew quiet and didn't want to play anymore.

She started getting bad grades in school and kept forgetting to do her homework.

On Saturday, Rosa went again to try and play with Susan. As she stood quietly by the gate, she saw Susan tightly holding her dog, Rowdy, and sobbing, "I don't want him do that anymore. I don't like him to touch me. Make it stop. Rowdy, make it stop!"

"Make what stop?" Rosa asked. Susan looked up in surprise! She hadn't seen her friend there.

"I can't tell you. My uncle said I better not tell anyone. He said no one would believe me, anyway."

"I will believe you, Susan. You know we share everything. And that includes Secrets!"

Susan whispered her Secret softly. "When my mom goes to work, my uncle comes in the bathroom to give me a bath. He touches me. Oh, Rosa, promise you won't tell anyone."

Rosa did promise her best friend she would keep her Secret, but all that day she didn't feel right about any of it.

When she went home, Rosa knew she should talk to her mother. They had a special place where they could talk about important things.

"Honey, is something the matter?" her mother asked. "Mommy, someone's touching Susan." "Who, Rosa?" her mother asked. "Her uncle. He just moved in with her and her mother. He gives her a bath at night when her mom goes to work and touches her."

"Did she tell you this?" her mother asked. "Yes, and she was crying too! What can we do mom?"

Rosa's mother held her tight. "Susan is old enough to take her own bath. Her uncle doesn't have the right to touch her like that. We are going to school tomorrow and talk with the school nurse. Susan is going to get the help she needs."

The next morning, Rosa was nervous as they talked with the school nurse. "We are worried about Rosa's best friend, Susan," her mother began. "She shared a Secret with Rosa that her uncle touches her when she is taking a bath."

The nurse looked tenderly at Rosa. She knew it was hard for her to break her promise to her best friend. "You're doing the right thing by sharing your friend's Secret," she told Rosa. "I'll see if Susan will talk with me."

Susan was scared when she was called to the nurse's office. "Susan, you're not in trouble, the nurse said. Let's go to a quiet room and talk for a while. Can you tell me a little about your home? Who lives with you, Susan?"

"My mom, and my uncle just moved in with us,"Susan said softly. "Does your mom work?" the nurse asked.

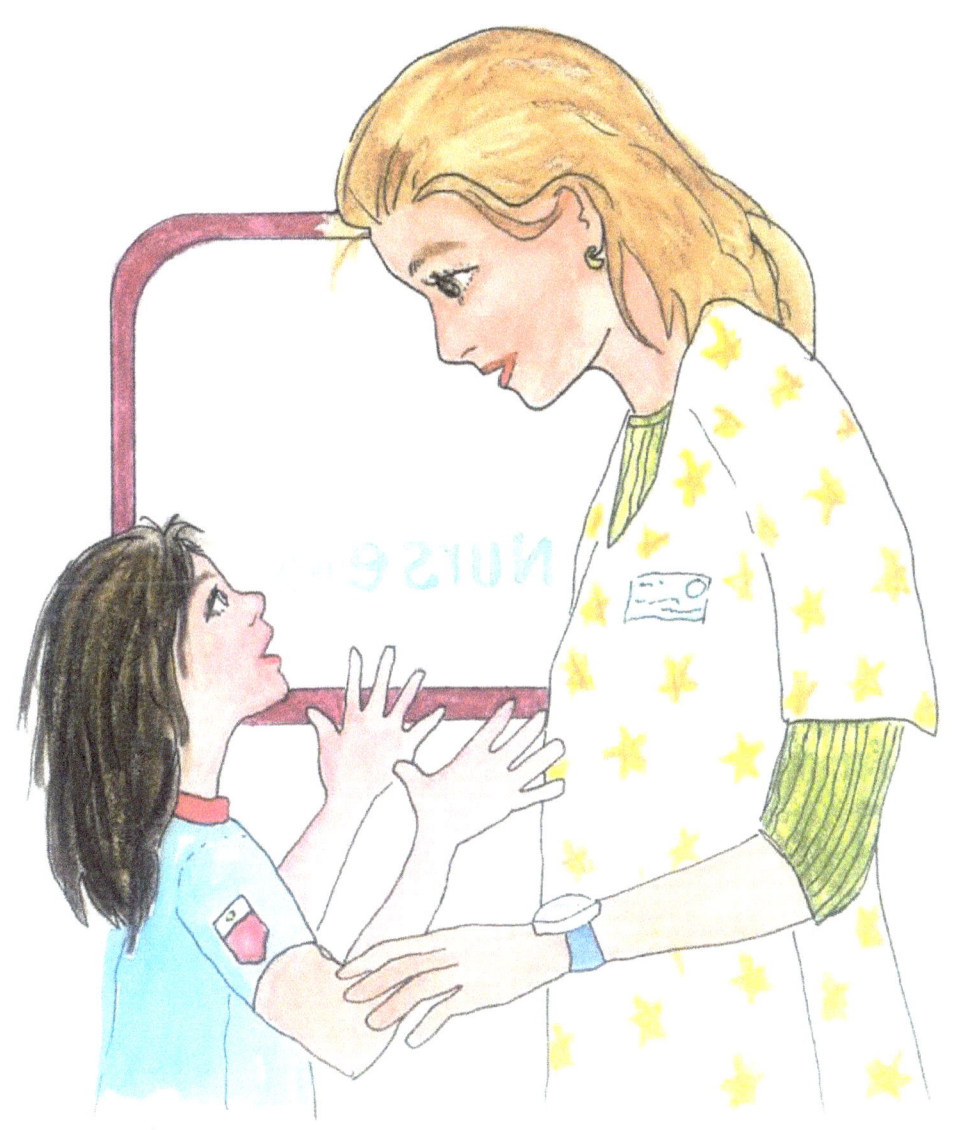

As Susan was telling the nurse about having to obey her uncle while her mother worked nights, she could no longer hold back the tears. "I don't like my mommy going to work," she sobbed.

"Susan, let's talk about what's making you cry." "I can't," Susan cried. "He said it's our Secret and no one will believe me."

"I believe you, Susan," the nurse said tenderly. "You are safe here."

Susan took a deep breath and spoke so softly the nurse could barely hear her. "My uncle touches me when I'm in the bathtub. I tell him 'no' but he won't stop!"

"Do you know what, Susan? I think you're a very brave girl to talk about this. It is not your fault. You've done nothing wrong. Your uncle doesn't have the right to touch you or be in the bathroom with you."

Susan buried her face in her hands, whispering between sobs. "I'm still afraid. My uncle pretends to be nice, but he's not. Please don't tell anyone."

The nurse could not promise that to Susan. It is the nurse's job to make reports to special people so children can be kept safe.

"Susan," the nurse said. "Everything is going to be okay. I'm going to get a counselor for you and your mother at the Center for Safe Child Services."

When Susan told her Secret to the people who help children, they believed her, and they were able to help her right away.

Before Susan and her mother even returned home, her uncle was gone. He couldn't visit either. Susan's counselor helped her to understand she did nothing wrong. Her mother learned to be on the lookout for signs that show children may be hiding a Secret.

One beautiful Sunday afternoon while Rosa and her mother were making their famous gingerbread cookies, there was a knock at the door.

Rosa ran to open the door.

"Susan!" "Rosa!" they both cried at the same time, hugging each other.

Susan's mother came to visit too. She knelt down beside Rosa. "I felt so bad that I didn't know what was happening to my daughter, Susan. Thank you for speaking up for her. You did the right thing by telling the Secret Susan shared with you."

"Terrible secrets are being kept by children everywhere. We have to let them know it is safe to tell. Only then can they get help."

Susan was quiet for a long time. Then she smiled!

"Rosa", she said, do you want to build a fort with me in the backyard?"

"Yes! Yes!" Rosa said. "My best friend is back!"

SUSAN SPEAKS TODAY

I hope my story will help other children who may be keeping a Secret. I thought I was the only person in the world with this kind of Secret.

I felt scared and so ashamed. Most children think they did something wrong.

This is not true. It is not your fault.

At first I thought no one would believe me. There are people who can help you, but you have to tell someone.

If you have a Secret like this, you cannot keep it to yourself. You have to ask for help.

I will take your hand and lead you to those who can help and together we will say "ENOUGH – THAT IS ENOUGH, LET'S END IT HERE AND NOW."

You can do it!

Susan

Hotline for "From Darkness to Light" 1 800-FOR LIGHT

DARKNESS TO LIGHT

The authors are in the greatest gratitude to the organization **From Darkness to Light** for their permission to include and make reference to their organization. Approximately one out of 10 children will be sexually abused before the age of 18. Only a third of these cases are identified and even less are reported.

In Mommy, Someone's Touching Susan, children are encouraged to tell someone about the child sexual abuse that is happening to them or someone they know. As concerned adults, it's important that we be there to listen to the child, provide support and know the steps to report abuse if appropriate. We at Darkness to Light encourage all adults to be trained in child sexual abuse prevention so they are able to respond appropriately when they are that trusted adult.

Darkness to Light offers an evidence informed program that trains adults how to prevent, recognize and react responsibly to child sexual abuse.

If you need help, are concerned about a child or adult's behavior, please call the Darkness to Light hotline at 1-866-FOR-LIGHT or visit www.D2L.org

ABOUT THE AUTHORS

Judith and Sandra have been best friends for many years. They worked together at an inner-city school in Phoenix, AZ. They have written a story to be the voice for Susan and children like her who are victims of child abuse.

Judith McClure is a retired teacher, published author and artist. She lives in White Springs, FL where she welcomes guests at her Bed and Breakfast.

Sandra Moyle is currently employed as a nurse in the Mental Health Field in Prescott, AZ. She worked 16 years as a school nurse and is sensitive and knowledgeable to the rising number of child abuse cases. She enjoys the outdoors, hiking, kayaking, and writing poetry.

ILLUSTRATOR

Sandy Lindfors majored in art at the University of Minnesota. She was employed as a graphic artist and illustrator for Palm Beach County Schools. Although retired, she is busy pursuing many artistic adventures.